MW01280150

# THE POWER OF MENTORSHIP

# THE MOVIE

*"Unlock Your Journey To Success"*

www.ThePowerOfMentorship.com
www.DonBoyer.org
www.DonBoyerAuthor.com

donboyer@realifeteaching.com

# The Power of Mentorship - The Movie

The Power of Mentorship - The Movie
Unlock Your Journey to Success

Published by Real Life Teaching/Publishing
donboyer@realifeteaching.com
www.DonBoyer.org
www.DonBoyerAuthor.com
www.ThePowerOfMentorship.com
562-789-1909
Whittier, California

Cover Design by Mick Moore
www.killerGraffix.com
Editing, Composition, and Typography by Paulette Bethel
www.ProEditingService.com

This book is available at quantity discounts for bulk purchase.
For more information, contact: Real Life Teaching/Publishing
donboyer@realifeteaching.com
Telephone: 562-789-1909
Whittier, California

Special Note: This edition of "The Power of Mentorship - The Movie" is designed to provide information and motivation to our readers. It is sold with the understanding that the publisher is not engaged to render any type of psychological, legal, or any other kind of professional advice. The content of each article is the sole expression and opinion of its author, and not necessarily that of the publisher. No warranties or guarantees are expressed or implied by the publisher's choice to include any of the content in this volume. Neither the publisher nor the individual author(s) shall be liable for any physical, psychological, emotional, financial, or commercial damages, including but not limited to special, incidental, consequential, or other damages. Our view and rights are the same: You are responsible for your own choices, actions, and results.

Printed in the United States of America

## Acknowledgement

A few days after I had seen the final cut of our movie project, I found myself overwhelmed with emotion. I sat there in awe as I realized I was not overwhelmed with emotion because of the movie, but because of the sense of pride in our team that made this film and book happen. I realized that the movie project was like a Lewis and Clark Expedition; I pushed my team to its limits, exhorting them to cross over rivers, mountains and valleys under the most extreme weather conditions.

Every one of our team members gave it everything they had and then some. They all did their very best and at the end of the journey my joy and happiness shot through the roof because I knew my team had given their all for this project. I love and appreciate every one of you. You are my heroes and you are giants in the land of the great. My team is as follows:

Our Lord, for creating all the abundance on this earth and making it a friendly universe so that mankind can be, do and have anything they desire.

My wife, Melinda, who is priceless and a true gift from God. Thank you for being my best friend, business partner, wife and soulmate.

Mick Moore, my wing man, partner and closest friend. I could not have done this project without you. You were our eyes, hands, brains, guard, general and genius behind this project. Your talents are those of the greatest artist in the history of the world. Thank you for being there all the way and taking care of business.

David Scandyln, you are one of a kind! You did your best; you stepped up to the plate and never gave up. Thank you for what you brought to this project.

Paul Robie. Thank you for believing in us and choosing to be part of our team and for your talents and studio. I will forever be grateful for what you did for us.

Dr. Letitia Wright. Thank you for being there from the very start. Your hand in this project made it fun and exciting.

Michael Harold, for your wonderful work in composing the music. It is music that heals the soul.

Bob Proctor, thank you for saying yes to being on this project, for your life changing message and for believing in me. It is an honor to call you my mentor.

Vic Johnson, you were the first to say yes when I started this project. From the day we met to the present, you have always given me support and help. Thank you being part of my dream.

Marie Diamond, thank you for the wonderful friendship you have given Melinda and me. You helped open doors that led to the success of this project. Thank you for your wisdom, love and insight.

Paulette Bethel, for taking on this project on short notice, for your editing skills and for always having faith in this project. Your talent is awesome!

To the entire cast members for bringing your message to the world and for your faith in this project, thank you:
Tony Alessandra
Marcia Wieder
Mick Moore
Gerry Robert
Paul Martinelli

Glenda Feilen
Lisha and Kari Schneider
Robin Jay
DC Cordova
Dr. John Demartini
Marc Accetta
Yasmine Bijan
Stephen and Lisa DiSalvio
Machen MacDonald
Dr. Marvin Pantangco
Peter Pizor
Dave and Yvette Ulloa
Ismael Perez
Christian Abrokwah
George Ramirez

To our crew:
Michael Natula
Eddie Barreiro
Lina Barker
Paul and Roberta Lauderdale

To our sponsors:
Terry Hall
Glenda Feilen
Lisha and Kari Schneider

# Foreword

**You may think this is just another book… it's not!
It's a treasure chest of information;
a life map to get you everything
you have always wanted in life.**

What was the secret that Beethoven, Einstein, Lincoln, Carnegie, Churchill, Ford, Firestone and Rockefeller had that caused them to create such phenomenal success? Was it education, family, good fortune, timing or just plain good luck? The answer is found in the secret they knew and understood. What was that secret? It's the Eight Laws of Success.

The truth of the matter is, the greatest successes and the vilest of failures are due to these great laws. The Eight Laws of Success are not some strange new-age method of thinking, but the very foundational laws of how life works on this planet. They are no different in operation or origin than the law of gravity or the law of physics.

We use the Eight Laws of Success everyday. However, most people do not know or understand these laws and therefore use them to bring to themselves the things they don't want instead of the things they do want.

Most people have a list of things they want and find they do not have. On the other hand, they have an even longer list of things that they do not want, yet find those are the things they do have. How hard did you try to get things messed up in your life? Did you wake some morning and think, "Ok, how am I going to screw up my life…what can I do to cause turmoil in my life?"

No, you didn't do that, yet you find that is the exact condition you face.

How did that happen? Many people will blame their spouse, job, family, education, or the government. But the truth of the matter is those things came by the Law of Attraction. By not understanding how the Law of Attraction works and implementing it, by default you get the results you don't want instead of the results you do want…think about that one for a moment!

The law that made Bill Gates one of the wealthiest men in the world is the same law that put Willie the Wino on skid row. It is the same law, just used in a different way. The Law of Attraction can make you rich or make you poor, keep you safe or open you up to trouble. It all depends on how you use it.

The good news is you are the master and ruler of the Eight Laws of Success. You get to control and govern them. You are the one who decides if these laws will work for you or against you. You govern them to bring you everything you want in life, or everything you don't want. That is the amazing thing about these eight laws. They are the Master Keys to life.

In this book, you will find the authors sharing various aspects of the Eight Laws to help you not only understand them, but how to apply them so they work to bring you everything you want in life. The truth of the matter is, you can be more, do more and have more...it's really up to you. The Eight Laws of Success, like the law of gravity, are impartial. They work for everybody, every time, everywhere.

They do not judge based on gender, race, age or status in life, they are immutable laws that work. The Eight Laws of Success really are like a genie who says, "Your wish is my command".

The Eight Laws do not think nor judge; if you put the command in, it doesn't matter if that request will benefit or hurt you, they bring it. The reason it is set up this way is because you are in charge. You are the Captain. You get to govern these laws however you choose.

It is one of the greatest gifts you were ever given when you hit planet earth. Unfortunately, most people were never told this secret, nor instructed on how to use these laws correctly. Once you understand how the Eight Laws of Success work, and begin to use them the correct way, you will see everything in your life change for the better.

You don't have to struggle with lack, sickness, unhappiness, loneliness or anything else that brings grief to your life. You can have an abundant life, filled with riches, happiness, fulfillment, excitement and everything else that will bring you pleasure. This right belongs to you, you already possess it.

And now you can start to experience it, once you apply the Eight Laws of success to your life.

May this book bring Freedom to Billions!

Master Mentors —
The Power of Mentorship Movie

The Power of Mentorship - The Movie

When you
**Dream**
you will have the
**Desire**
to have a clear
**Vision**
for
**Right Thinking.**
The
**Law of Attraction**
Will help you find the right
**Associations**
for you to take
**Action**
So that you can
**Believe**
in your dreams.

The Power of Mentorship - The Movie

# Table of Contents

Introduction                              17

The 8 Laws                                19

Chapter 1  Dream                          21

Chapter 2  Desire                         31

Chapter 3  Vision                         41

Chapter 4  Right Thinking                 49

Chapter 5  Law of Attraction             61

Chapter 6  Associations                  69

Chapter 7  Action                        79

Chapter 8  Believe                       87

Chapter 9  Power of Mentorship           97

Bob Proctor Summary                      99

Bonus Chapters                          101

The Next Step by Don Boyer              109

Master Mentor Biographies               115

The Power of Mentorship - The Movie

# Introduction

## Who You Listen to Will
## Determine Your Future...

In this true story of a young man and his mentor you will find the golden keys that will help you unlock your journey to success. It is the hybrid of a moving story, coupled with an informative documentary of 27 Master mentors such as Bob Proctor, Marie Diamond, Vic Johnson, Tony Alessandra, Glenda Feilen, Lisha and Kari Schneider, Melinda Boyer and Mick Moore. It has the power to bring freedom to billions.

Explore the depths to unlocking the millionaire code within you and learn how to use the Law of Attraction to bring you everything you desire. Featuring eight powerful Laws that can transform your life into the magnificent creation it is designed to be, the Master mentors teach you...

- The only difference between a rich man and a poor man is his method of thinking
- There is an easy way and a hard way to life

- Only those who know how to peer into the invisible can do the impossible
- What we believe within determines what we have without
- You were born rich and all things belong to you

Included in this book is a bonus chapter, a special message from Don Boyer, outlining you the next step to success.

Get out your yellow marker, pen and paper and jot down the Keys that will unlock your journey to success. From Janitor to Business Entrepreneur…I did it, so can you!

Now, go find yourself a mentor.

# The Eight Laws

### Dream
A dream is that burning feeling you have on the inside that you feel compelled to bring to the outside... now that is a dream.

### Desire
Desire is the jet fuel for your dreams. It is what gives you the power to take action on those dreams.

### Vision
Vision is not a function of eyesight but of the imagination. Only those who can peer into the invisible can do the impossible.

### Right Thinking
The only difference between a rich man and a poor man is his method of thinking. A poor man thinks on things he does not want and a rich man thinks on things he does want.

## Law of Attraction

The Law of Attraction is the great force that brings everything into our life. Good, bad or indifferent; it all comes to us by this great Law. This Law can bring you everything you ever desired in life.

## Associations

Who you surround yourself with and listen to will determine what you get, what you have and where you go in life. Associations determine your future.

## Action

Action is what takes things out of the invisible realm and translates them into the physical realm. Tell me what your results are and I will tell you what your actions have been.

## Believe

Faith is your ability to see into the invisible so that you can grasp onto that which is incredible and be able to go out and do what the masses say is impossible.

# Chapter One

## Dream

Walk down any busy street or look at a crowded freeway and you will find people that are frustrated, confused and without hope. Today, millions of people around the globe got up to go to a job they do not like, working for a paycheck that does not meet their financial needs and only stifles their creativity.

**In life, there is an easy way or a hard way...**
**Unfortunately, most are doing it the hard way.**

In 1979, I was 19 years old. I was a janitor when I met the mentor who forever changed my life. The following is based on a true story.

**The day Alonzo meets his Mentor**

Alonzo, a bright 19 year old, is a young man who has a crisp mind and great potential but, because he started his family at 17, was unable to finish his formal education. The only way he can support his family is by cleaning office buildings.

Struggling with financial lack, yet surrounded by people who live in abundance in the office building he cleans, he dreams of the day he, too, can be successful.

As Alonzo settles into his daily work mode he finds himself once again discouraged with his lot in life. Suddenly, he realizes Mr. Boyer, the company president, is still in his office working, "Oh, hi, Mr. Boyer, I didn't realize you were still here. Mind if I dump your trash?"

As Alonzo begins to empty the trash, his mind races with the thought of what it must be like to be a successful business entrepreneur. The thought is so strong, it gives him the courage to ask, "Can I ask you a question?"

Mr. Boyer looks up from his paperwork and replies, "Sure Alonzo, what's on your mind?"

Taking a deep breath, Alonzo asks, "How did you become so successful?"

Intrigued by the question, Mr. Boyer looks deep into the eyes of the young man standing in front of him. It is a look so probing that Alonzo feels as though his soon-to-be mentor is looking into his soul.

22

The president says, "Alonzo, success is more a journey than a destination. There are eight things you will need to help you along this journey or pathway.

"Come over here. Take a seat."

"Eight things," Alonzo blurts out, "that seems like a lot!"

Mr. Boyer smiles within, remembering how he, as a young man, had those very thoughts when his mentor told him about the Eight Laws of Success.

"You know, Alonzo, about 97 percent of all people have that same kind of mind set, and that is why they never accomplish their dreams or do much in life. If you really want to be successful, the first thing you need is a *Dream*. And a *Dream* is not wishful thinking, but a burning desire you feel deep inside. It is so intense that you feel compelled to get it out. Now, that's a *dream.*"

## Master Mentors on Dream

### Yasmine Bijan – Business Success Coach

*Dreams are your jet fuel to strive in your life. Usually, fueling your dreams comes from passion and purpose. When you live your life from passion and purpose you experience so much more joy, peace and satisfaction in your life. Dreams require a team to make them happen. So remember, Dreams take a team.*

### Melinda Boyer, CEO – Real Life Teaching  Inc.

*Your dreams are your road map to success. When you are dreaming of the impossible it is only you that can make it manifest in your life; you have to feel it in your heart and see it with your eyes to really make it possible… So tell me, what is it that you are dreaming?*

### George Ramirez – Professional Speaking Coach

*Dreams are really important; the dream that is inside of you. Each of us, by design, has a dream that will pull us through the tough times in our lives. Our dreams have a purpose. That is why it is so important and so exciting; it is there so that we can help the world. When we live out our dreams, the world benefits. Today, I am living my dream. I am in awe of where I am. But you know, I had a dream and I am living it. I encourage you to do the same.*

### Robin Jay – Motivational Speaker

*Don't ever let the dream stealers diminish or weaken your dream in any way. Sometimes, well intentioned family members and friends have a tendency to keep us pigeon- holed in the roles that they see us in. Once you share your dreams with them, they may see a lot of ways that it will not work out for you. They want to share this with you so that you won't get your hopes up. Well, life has some disappointments in it.*

*Once you achieve one dream it is so much easier to achieve the next dream and the next and before long you're living your dream everyday.*

*Remember to put a deadline on your dreams because that transforms into a goal. Once you set a goal it is a lot easier to get there.*

### Marcia Wieder, Founder – DreamUniversity.com

*Dreams come from you; you make them up. Some of them are based on need, like putting food on the table; some are based on desire, what is truly in your heart. But the dreams that are usually most profound, are the ones that are the expression of your purpose or your mission.*

*The difference between a dream and a fantasy like winning the lottery, is that in a dream you can design a strategy for getting there. In my travels around the world, I have found it is not that people never go to strategy; it is that they tend to go there too soon. We compromise our dreams down.*

### *Marie Diamond – Feng Shui Master*
*Dreaming is not about a fantasy world; it is about creating your own reality. Dreaming is actually expressing the deepest part of you, what it is you have come here to do. This comes forward in your dreaming but you can't just stay with the dream in your fantasy world. You must make that dream a reality.*

*So go inside yourself, feel it in your soul and feel it in your deeper self, what you are really here to do. What is your vision? What is your dream to accomplish? Don't create anything else than what you are here to do; just focus on it. Live that dream from the moment you start your day, until the moment you finish your day. I can tell you by living it and believing it, you attract it.*

### *Marc Accetta, CEO – Marc Accetta Seminars*
*During my first serious relationship, I remember coming home one day and my girlfriend sat me down and really let me have it. She said to me, as if I was the lowest form of existence on the planet, "You are such a dreamer!"*

*And I knew right then that the relationship had to end. Because to me, if you are not dreaming, you're not alive. As time has gone on I have realized that every successful person I have studied has been a dreamer.*

*When Walt Disney was in grade school he had a teacher that ridiculed him and told him that flowers didn't have faces. Imagine someone trying to limit Walt Disney's dreams. Just look at what he did and the dynasty that he created. I wonder how that teacher feels these days.*

*The bottom line is that Walt Disney said it better then anyone. "If you can dream it, you can do it."*

**Vic Johnson, Founder – AsAManThinketh.net**
*The Roman Emperor Marcus Aurelius said, "Dream big dreams. Only big dreams have the power to move men's souls."*

*In 1987, not too far from where we are today, a discouraged and depressed comedian who had had a rough night, got in his old Toyota and drove up Mulholland Drive to the top of the Hollywood Hills.*

*He sat there looking over the city at that view we have seen so many times in motion pictures, and thought about his life. He took out one of his personal checks* *and made it out to himself for $10 million dollars. He dated it Thanksgiving, 1995.*

*In the memo section he wrote, 'For acting services rendered'. He tore the check out of his check book and stood there and looked at it, and he dreamed of the day that it would be real.*

*That was the dream he had; the dream that he carried. He stuck that check in his wallet and every time, in the days ahead when times would get rough and when the audiences would boo him and it seemed like he would never live his dream, he would pull that check out and look at it. That is what kept him going.*

*Jim Carey had been pretty conservative that night because by the time Thanksgiving 1995 rolled around, he wasn't making $10 million dollars a movie, he was making $20 million a movie.*

*As James Allen says, in* As A Man Thinketh *"Dream lofty dreams and as you dream so shall you become."*

### Bob Proctor, Best Selling Author –
You Were Born Rich
*You have got to have a dream. If you do not have a dream, how are going to make your dream come true?*

*Do you know where dreams start? Dreams start by fantasizing.*

*Now think of this for a moment; when you were a little child you were encouraged to fantasize but then, when you went to school, they called it day dreaming and not paying attention and—bang!—we had a lid put on it.*

*Well, take the lid off and get your imagination going! Let's fantasize! Let's sit down and relax and ask ourselves, "What do I really want to do? What do I really want to do with my life?" Build your dream in your mind.*

*You see, your imagination is a mental faculty. It is one of the highest faculties you have. It is what helps you get in touch with what is going on inside.*

*We have got to stop living just with our five senses; quit going by what we hear, see, smell, taste, touch. Go by that inner eye of understanding. Fantasize!*

*Ask yourself, "What do I really want?"*

*I have a magnificent dream in my mind all the time. It is what keeps me going. And this is what will keep you going. Sit down and forget about what the world tells you you can do. What is it that you want to do?*

*It was a dream that got Edmund Hillary to the top of Mt. Everest. Everyone said it could not be done. But he believed it could be done. He was an ordinary bee keeper in Auckland, New Zealand. Where did he get this idea? He got it from the infinite, he dreamed it.*

*Stop and think about the Wright Brothers, a couple of bicycle mechanics, in Dayton, Ohio. The whole world said that anything heavier than air is attracted to the center of the world. We can not fly! But we have. And do you know it took four years before people believed that they really got planes in the air?*

*Now think about it. They believed it because they dreamed it. Someone said that they were listening to a song. "Birds fly over a rainbow, why oh why then, can't I?"*

*And that is what put us in the air. It was a dream that got them up there. It is a dream that is going to transform your life. Fantasize, build a big picture in your consciousness and then really pay attention to what everyone in this film is saying. They will show you how to turn a dream into a physical reality.*

# Chapter Two

## Desire

As Alonzo is absorbing all the information about what a *dream* is he is brought back to the present by Mr. Boyer's voice penetrating the air saying, "The next thing you need after your *Dream* is *Desire.*" The best way I can explain it is to say desire is like jet fuel for your dream. It gives you the power and ability to take action on your dream.

## Master Mentors on Desire

### Dr Letitia Wright – Wright Place TV Show Host
*Your real desires come to your mind often. You don't have to put anything on the mirror to remind yourself; they will keep coming back over and over again. And they will give you motivation.*

### Dave Ulloa – Business Entrepreneur
*It all starts with a burning desire. Back in high school I had a burning desire to play professional basketball. I had no clue how I was going to do it and, only standing 5'8" tall, I was not the most likely to be a professional athlete.*

*I remember all through high school and college many people would tell me I couldn't make it to the next level. It wasn't that they didn't love me; they just didn't want me to get my hopes up. What if I failed? That would have been a major disappointment.*

*What kept me on course was that dream—the burning desire that I had—it basically kept me up late at night and woke me up early in the morning. I ate, slept and drank basketball. And I am proud to say that eight years later, I was very blessed to play professional basketball for several years. It all started with a burning desire.*

**George Ramirez – Professional Speaking Coach**
*Desire! Let me tell you about desire. Inside desire there is a rebar called inspiration and it is that which is encouragement for you; to do what many would consider absolutely impossible.*

*I will share with you the best example I can about desire. Before my wife became my wife, I was working on her to become my girlfriend. She and her family were going on their annual vacation for two weeks in Yosemite. Now, I was 438 miles away from Yosemite, and the thought of not seeing her for two weeks…, that was not going to work for me.*

*I knew I could not drive because my car wouldn't have made it to Yosemite even if it was downhill all the way. So I grabbed a duffle bag, threw in a sleeping bag, a few toiletries and whatever money I could scrounge up. That afternoon I found myself at the major intersection in the little town that I lived in. I had my thumb out, hitchhiking!*

*The concept of getting there? Not a problem. I was on my way to Yosemite. How? I didn't care; all I knew was that I was getting there.*

*11 hours later, about 2:30 in the morning, I was pulling into the parking space across from her campsite. I thought to myself, "I got here in 11 hours without a plan."*

*So what is the big deal? Desire will enable you to do the amazing. Get hold of your desire. You can do it.*

### Marcia Wieder, Founder– DreamUniversity.com

*I have seen people sometimes go further in life because of their desire and commitment than with skill, experience, or even gobs of money.*

*I met a young man, Wilson. He told me he was from Kenya, Africa. He was part of the Maasai Warrior Tribe and I met him in Portland. When I asked him what he was doing there, he told me that as a young child it had always been his dream to become a doctor but there was no place to get trained in Africa and you didn't leave the tribe. It just wasn't done.*

*He shared his dream with everyone and they would roll their eyes and tell him it was just a fantasy and to forget it. But he never did, and around his 18th birthday a writer came to visit. It turned out that this guy worked for the* Washington Post. *He wrote about Wilson's desire and a couple in Portland happened to read it. Within a matter of weeks he was invited to apply for undergraduate work and within a month was accepted to the University of Portland.*

*I said to him "That's extraordinary" and he said, "No, Marcia, at that point it was horrific because this amazing opportunity was being presented to me but we didn't have the resources to send me off to America.*

*So I did the only thing I knew how to do; I prayed for a miracle. I used my deep desire and you know, this is what I got."*

### Dr. Marvin Pantangco – Health Expert
*Once you have visualized your dream, the very next step you have to take is to find your desire. Now where do you find desire? Do you find it at the store or can you buy it over the internet?*

*You find it in your heart! Everyone has desire. Everyone has a strong desire to win, and everyone has a strong desire to conquer their fears.*

*The Great Napoleon Hill said it best, "When your desires are strong enough you will appear to possess superhuman powers to achieve."*

### Glenda Feilen – Life Improvement Specialist
*Desire is where you go with your heart. When you have a desire you feel it right down in the pit of your stomach. As it gets stronger it begins to move and, for some, it becomes a burning in your bosom. Then*

*it moves up into your throat. Pretty soon, you just have to tell someone and when you do they will catch the spark! Some even get enlightened and want to help you.*

*Fulfill your desire because all of your desires are coming out of you. The universe sends creative ideas and when you take action on those ideas, the activity you do is not exhausting; it is refreshing, invigorating. Why? Because you are doing what you love! Because you love what you do! You are doing your heart's desire.*

### Melinda Boyer, CEO – Real Life Teaching Inc.

*If there is a desire that you are passionate about and you can visualize and see yourself doing whatever you desire, take the steps that are necessary to get there. It just takes one step at a time for whatever your heart really desires.*

*Back in 1989, I was working for a finance company and really wanted to get to the executive level. I was working as a temp in the data entry department at the time, and saw myself at the executive level. But there were steps that I needed to take in order to get there.*

*The steps were that I had to surround myself with the executives and auditors and whoever else was working on the 10th floor where the executives were. I had to understand that I needed to put myself into that position, go back to school, and understand what the executive were really all about.*

*If there is one desire that you are passionate about, and you can envision yourself there—whatever your desire is—then start taking the steps that are necessary to get there; just one step at a time to get whatever your heart really desires. The truth is, we always get what we truly desire. So think about what your desires are and just go for it!*

**Lisha & Kari Schneider – Networking Specialists**
**Kari** *– Desire is the key to motivation, the key to commitment and the key to any success you want to have. When you have desire, everything is possible; you become unlimited.*

**Lisha** *– Nothing happens by chance. When you have a strong desire the law of cause and effect comes into play in your life; desire is the cause and the effect is the result of your desire.*

**Kari** *– When you have a strong enough desire, it puts a particular vibration into the universe and it is an absolute law that it must come back to you*

**Lisha** – *Know what you want to create, and then become the vibrational match for it, and receive it! You will do this if you have a strong enough desire.*

### Bob Proctor, Best Selling Author –
You Were Born Rich

*You know, I have listened to sales managers and vice presidents of sales for years, and they would say, if I could only build a desire into some of these people. And you know, generally, these people that this was being told to had no idea what they were saying.*

*What is desire? It comes from the Latin: to give birth to the children. Desire is the idea that you build in your conscious and turn over to your subconscious, and desire is the dream that is cooking in your universal subconscious mind; your emotional mind.*

*"Desire," Wallace Wattles from* The Science of Getting Rich *said, "is the effort of the unexpected possibility within, seeking expectation without, through your actions."*

*Desire is the yeast that raises the dough. Desire is the gas in the engine. Without desire you are never going to do more than you are doing right now.*

*How do we get it? We build a dream and we let ourselves get emotionally involved with it. We live it! It is called image reality.*

*Become an actor; think about how they do it. They get the script, they read the script, they memorize the script, they internalize the script and they become the script. This is how you build desire. Don't listen to the people around you, Don't listen to the nay sayers.*

*Remember, there is a very small percentage of the population that makes things happens. You are going to make things happen, and you make things happen because you are taking your dream and getting emotionally involved with it.*

*Get that desire going; you will love what it does to you.*

The Power of Mentorship - The Movie

# Chapter Three

## Vision

"You know," Alonzo said as his mind raced, "I have had that feeling before, I just didn't know what it was."

"That was your dream mixed with desire, Alonzo. Ok, now that you have your dream and desire, you need vision. And vision is not of the eyes but of the mind. You see, eyesight is limited, but your imagination... well, that's unlimited.

"You know, it was one of our greatest thinkers that said, 'Only those who can see the invisible can do the impossible.'"

## *Master Mentors on Vision*

### *Machen MacDonald – Achievement Expert*
*Well, I think vision answers two questions. First Question: Where are we going? Second Question: Who are we becoming?*

*The great thing about this is that we get a chance to make it up. Most people are making up a tired vision and this is not an inspired vision. You see, it is our thoughts and actions that drives our visions, which gets us to the feeling that we will feel. And it is our emotion which drives our actions, and our actions takes care of our results.*

*So, if you want good results, you have to have great thoughts. If you are not concerned about the results, let your thoughts go where they may.*

### *Dr. Peter J. Pizor – Author*
*Have you ever been rock climbing and you climb up the cliff and you get to a certain point and you become stuck right where you are? You were successful because you have made it half way up, but you haven't reached your goal. You are not sure what to do, and you can't let go but the guide tells you let go! You are thinking to yourself, if I let go I am going to fall!*

*Sometimes we are stuck in our minor successes and those minor successes keep us from reaching the top. The secret is to clear a space for your vision, let go of the little things that are holding on to you so you can reach up and find that great hole and pull yourself up to the summit. That is where the vision is.*

***George Ramirez – Professional Speaking Coach***
*The part about vision that is so amazing is that it allows you to be creative about your desired end result. That is why vision is so critical. Let me share with you what happened to me.*

*When I was leaving one business for another, in that transitional time I just didn't want to not show up. I wanted to leave with integrity for those people I had been working with. So on January the 7th, during the annual goal setting time, I stood up to speak and, in front of my peers, 65 to 70 of them, I thanked them for a great experience and encouraged them for the new year and said "Good Bye".*

*I told them, 'I walked in here with my head up, I am leaving with my head up. I wish you the best.' When I did this there was a moment of silence and then they stood up and acknowledged me and gave me a standing ovation because I had the vision to believe I could leave with integrity. You can do anything you want! Vision creates what you want!*

### Robin Jay – Motivational Speaker

*Make sure your vision is crystal clear and imagine what everyday is going to be like. When my brother was in college, he was doing everything he could to get into the California School of Psychology.*

*The Dean finally told him that he was in, congratulations, but he had one more question for my brother. Why would a positive, self actualized individual like you want to surround yourself with negative self destructive people every single day?*

*My brother's answer was, "I think I can create an environment for people that would help them move forward and heal."*

*But he had never really thought about what his day to day existence would be like. As he left his interview on the 4th floor of building he got down to the second tier in the stair well and he sat down and put his head in his hands and started to cry.*

*Because he had worked so hard toward this vision and goal he had never realized what each day was really going to be like. He ended up changing direction.*

*So make sure that your vision is crystal clear in every way. What is it going to be like every day, every week and every month?*

### Lisa Mason DiSalvo – Motivational Speaker
*Pick a vision of something that you will be passionately committed to; that you absolutely love where you want it to go.*

*It is kind of like building a puzzle; when you build a puzzle you pick the picture because it's beautiful, it's peaceful, it's challenging and it's motivating. Do the same for your vision and then, just like when you look at the picture of the puzzle to help guide your next step, look at your vision. Take time everyday to look at it and ponder on it; pondering on it will guide you to your next steps.*

### Stephen DiSalvio – Motivational Speaker
*All accomplishments start with a vision. Take the architect; the architect who is creating a building starts out with rough sketches and they blossom into a fantastic piece of architecture that's all his. He is then left with a beautiful finished product.*

*Everyone needs to have a vision; without vision you can't get started. If you can't get started, you cannot go after a goal. Get crystal clarity in your mind, get your vision in your mind and go for it.*

### Yasmine Bijan – Business Success Coach
*Vision is something that you cannot see with your physical eye. With your physical eye you can actually*

*see something around you; that would be vision. The minds eye has a vision for something that is in your imagination. Powerful leaders have vision and with that vision they engage everyone around them to move toward their vision. Through that vision you want to articulate to as many people as you possibly can so your vision is able to come into fruition.*

### Glenda Feilen – Life Improvement Specialist
*It is important to have a vision in your mind, but it is just as important to see your vision in your mind. Your mind thinks in pictures. When you have a thought, your conscious mind changes it to a mental picture. Psychologists tell us that these pictures are one of our strongest mind powers and you can use these inner visions to change your life.*

*Create specific situations that you want to manifest in your life and experience them just as if they were happening to you right now. With your inner vision use these mental images to resolve family and relationship problems, to change your finances, to create healing.*

*No one will ever change their life until they see themselves with their inner vision in a different role.*

## Bob Proctor, Best Selling Author –
You Were Born Rich

*You know, it has been said by every great leader that has ever lived; you have got to have a vision, you have got to have a picture, a long range view of where you are going to go.*

*I see vision almost like an image that flows from my consciousness and goes out and gets broader and brighter and farther away. It's the long range picture of what we're going to do with our lives. I have my vision and you have yours. It is a multiplicity of things that you want to happen.*

*Do you know what really builds a vision in your mind? It's a strong desire to make something happen that is greater than what is happening in your life. It's a long range picture.*

*You see, you build your purpose; that is why you are living and your vision is how you are going to execute your purpose. It is a multiplicity of goals that you see way out in front of you. You don't know how it is going to happen, but you know it is going to happen. It's the long range vision of what you are going to do in your life. Build that vision and then start moving toward it.*

The Power of Mentorship - The Movie

# Chapter Four

## Right Thinking

Alonzo's mind was spinning with ideas and concepts that he has never heard before. Somehow, they resonated in the depths of his soul as he explained to the company president, "I do understand what you are saying about vision, but how can I be a success? I mean, all I have is this job. I didn't go to high school. I don't have any money saved. How I am supposed to become successful?"

Mr. Boyer could feel his eyes wanting to mist over because he knew he was witnessing an individual who was striving to be more, do more and have more. With heart-felt compassion, he began, "Alonzo, you are using your imagination, but you are using it incorrectly. You are using your imagination to see all the things you don't have and all the things you are not.

"Start using your imagination to see all the things you do want and the things you can be.

"Let me ask you a question. Have you ever gotten something for Christmas that you really wanted?"

Alonzo pondered the question and then said, "Sure, I got a 10 speed bike once".

Using his wisdom and insight, Mr. Boyer tells Alonzo, "Two weeks before Christmas what did you do?"

"Well, I thought about that bike all the time and I even imagined myself riding it everyday," was Alonzo's reply.

"Exactly, Alonzo, that's it!" proclaimed Mr. Boyer. "That is using your imagination the right way. You saw yourself with something you wanted, you felt the emotion of having it and then you had it.

"You see, Alonzo, you can't think small and expect to live big, you can't think like a poor person and expect to live like a rich person. It does not work that way. My mentor told me that the only difference between a rich man and a poor man is his method of thinking.

"This leads us to our next principle which is that you have to learn how to think right. You have to learn to think correctly."

## *Master Mentors on Right Thinking*

### *Dave Ulloa – Business Entrepreneur*
*Ask yourself this question; what is thinking?*

*Well, when you really think about it, thinking is the process of asking and answering questions all day long. 'Why am I not successful?'*

*What your brain does is search for answers and it will respond that maybe we are not smart enough or are not good enough.*

*The flip side to that is what if we start to ask ourselves powerful questions like 'how can I become successful?'*

*Your brain will start searching for answers. It might suggest something like read a book such as* Think and Grow Rich, *or go into a personal development seminar, or maybe find a great mentor.*

*We must pay attention to the questions we ask ourselves, and really condition our mind to ask ourselves powerful questions that will take us in a direction we truly desire.*

### Dr. Peter J. Pizor – Author

*Have you ever been going along, lost in thought, and you turn a corner and there is the last person you want to see on the planet? Well, I have!*

*I was out for a run one day and there, larger than life, was my ex-wife. I walked past her and said "Hi!" She said "Hi", and as I went on I thought to myself, "Wait a second. I have been carrying two people on this run; myself and a memory."*

*Then I thought, "What is right thinking?" and I made a U-turn. My U-turn brought me back to her and I said, "How are you really doing?" and she said, "I am doing okay. How are you?" and we walked together for three miles and came to the parking lot where her car was parked.*

*I didn't know it but in that parking lot were two grandchildren who had never, in their entire life, seen their grandparents anywhere together. What I learned on that trip was when I let go of what I am carrying, I have space to connect with somebody and wonderful things open up.*

*Now, that is right thinking.*

## *Lisa Mason DiSalvo– Motivational Speaker*
*You really have to have a lot of right thinking. You need to have thoughts that are positive and that have energy and belief and confidence. Thoughts like 'what if' and 'I should have' and 'it won't work' are the negative thoughts that lead you into fear and anxiety.*

*The anxiety and fear lead you into not taking action, and then the not taking action leads you back into the negative thoughts, and then you are in this whirlwind cycle.*

*You need to find a way to break that cycle. Van Gogh once said, "If you hear a voice inside you say you cannot paint, then by all means, paint. And that voice will be silenced."*

*Find the voice inside you that tells you to paint.*

## *Dr. Marvin Pantangco – Health Expert*
*Thinking right is so important. Good health starts with positive thinking. Do this and you save a lot of precious time and energy, just by thinking positively. Do this and you will achieve everything you want in life.*

### Glenda Feilen – Life Improvement Specialist
*You have two minds: you have a conscious thinking mind that is awake when you are awake and you have a subconscious mind that is always awake but never thinks. This is the one that creates your reality. It has created the life that you have right now.*

*Life is not about finding yourself; life is about creating yourself. In order to do that, you have to take control of your mind. Thoughts are habits in your mind reproduced in your physical world. You are where you are because of your habits and thoughts. If you want to know what a person thinks about, look at his life. You can control your life and your future by controlling the thoughts you feed your creative or subconscious mind.*

### Yvette Ulloa – Business Entrepreneur
*Have you ever wondered what the difference is between a Michael Jordan and someone that is just comfortable with their life with minimal or no results? You got it! The difference is in their thinking patterns.*

*So, how is it that we create the right mind set? If we feed our mind positive things, coupled by the right action, we will have great results. However, if we feed our mind negative things, such as the news, disempowering things, frequencies that are negative,*

*negative friendships, then we will tune into a lower frequency with negative results.*

**Vic Johnson, Founder – AsAManThinketh.net**
*My thinking had created the terrible, terrible life that I seemed to lead at the time. And I know that there are people watching this that are in their own crisis and they can't imagine that they created it.*

*You see, we don't have control over anything in our life. We don't have control over our spouse, we don't have control over our children, for sure, we don't have control over our boss, we don't have control over the economy. The only thing we have control over is what we think using a technique called metacognition.*

*Now, that is a big word! It simply means, thinking about what you are thinking about. You do that on a regular basis and you create a different pattern of thinking, you create different thoughts.*

*Whatever you dwell on, you are going to expand in your life. When I was dwelling on lack I got a lot more lack. It is almost like the universe says, that's what Vic wants, let's give him some more of it. When I began to dwell on abundance, abundance was attracted to me.*

### Lisha & Kari Schneider – Networking Specialists

*Kari – Everything you have in life started with a thought; by you or someone else. Your thoughts create your life. Your mind automatically reacts to the thoughts you give it and takes action on exactly what you are thinking.*

*Lisha – What occupies your mind? Movies, video games, TV filled with violence? Just as a magnet attracts, your mind attracts material equivalent to its most frequent thoughts. That is why it is simply impossible for a negative mind to attract positive things.*

*Kari – Think of only what you want, not of what you don't want. When you worry about what you are going to get, you are going to get more of what you don't want. That is a very destructive habit. The good news is habits can be changed.*

*Lisha – Take charge of your thoughts and determine carefully what plays on your mind's stage. What plays on your mental stage will soon come to play on your life stage.*

### Bob Proctor, Best Selling Author –
You Were Born Rich

*You know, it is very important that you get on the right road to a bright future. Thinking is the highest function that the human person is capable of. The great and late educator, Dr. Ken McFarland said, "2% of the people think, 3% of the people think they think and 95% of people would rather die then think."*

*I remember Earl Nightingale said, "If most people said what they were thinking, they would be speechless." Now, you are probably sitting there saying, "Everybody thinks."*

*The truth is, very few people think. If you pay attention to what most people are doing it is obvious that they are not thinking, or they would never do what they are doing. Pay attention to what they are saying. They would never say what they are saying if they were thinking. I want you to begin to really think!*

*You see, mental activity does not constitute thinking. Your senses pick up actions that are going on around you. That is mental activity. But that is not thinking. There is a phenomenal power that flows to and through you and as it flows into your consciousness, you have a reasoning factor. It gives you the ability to build little pictures into your consciousness.*

*Because we think in pictures and we bring these pictures together, we build ideas. But we want to get involved in right thinking. That's the thought that is going to get you where you want to go.*

*It is easy to get involved in wrong thinking. That is when we are thinking why we can't do it, you see! If you knew how to do it, you would already be there.*

*The trick to life is to enjoy the trip, enjoy how you are going to do it, and you are going to enjoy doing that by right thinking.*

*I know I can! I know I can! I'm going to do it! And I just need to think how and one thought leads to other and one step leads to another and pretty soon the dreams and desires have manifested.*

*You have got to keep thinking the right way; don't listen to all the people around you. They are talking about why things can't be done.*

*Quit reading the daily newspaper, it is full of nothing but terrible things. You won't find good thoughts in the newspaper. Quit listening to the news.*

*Watch inspirational films, listen to inspirational CD's, read good books and pay attention to the people you are associating with. Get right thoughts flowing through your consciousness because it is going to change your life. That's what it will do!*

*Right thinking is vitally important.*

The Power of Mentorship - The Movie

# Chapter 5

## Law of Attraction

As the light begins to dawn in Alonzo's consciousness, he tells his mentor, "I am realizing that I can have more and be more. I am not limited like people said I was. I don't have to be a janitor all my life. By using these principles I can really reach my dreams."

With a wildly beating heart and awareness rushing through his body, Alonzo leans over and asks, "So, you are telling me that my thoughts create my reality? I actually get the things I think about?"

"Yes, Alonzo," proclaims his mentor, "and this is why the next principle is so important for you to understand. It is called the Law of Attraction. Everything we have in life; good, bad or indifferent, we brought to us with the Law of Attraction. Some people call this law the great secret to life."

## Mentors on The Law of Attraction

### Yasmine Bijan – Business Success Coach

*The Law of Attraction is based on what you focus upon, you expand upon. Like attracts like, so if that is the case, focus on your thoughts and your feelings and make sure that they align. Be a detective in your own life and figure out what is getting in the way of your producing results. Identify those subconscious negative beliefs.*

### Machen MacDonald – Achievement Expert

*We live in a universe that is made of vibrational matter or energy and the reality is that anything we want to do, be or have is out there and available to us. The challenge is that we are not making ourselves available to it.*

*Take joy for example; if we go out there and act more joyful we start to interact more with people who are joyful, we start to bring in more things that bring us joy and so the trick is to go out and feel that as much as you can and that will start to attract more of what you want for yourself.*

### DC Cordova – Money & You ®

*Look and see how you have attracted this magnificent teacher to you to help you. You must have had the thought that you wanted this; otherwise it would*

62

*have not happened. Who do you want to teach you more? Be clear, do your research, immerse yourself in these thoughts and they will be attracted into your life. Some of the most successful people in the world would love to help people like you.*

*A la gente com mas ventajas en el mundo les encenta ayudar personas como a ti.*

### Dr. Marvin Pantangco – Health Expert
*The Secret is, the Law of Attraction is no longer a secret. The fact that you are listening to me right now means that the Law of Attraction works. It's all around us. Whether you like it or not, it is there. What you think about, you attract. It is as simple as that.*

### Dr. Tony Alessandra, Author – The Platinum Rule
*My take on the Law of Attraction is a little different. It is interpersonal attraction; how you attract people to you. What I propose is The Platinum Rule as opposed to the Golden Rule.*

*The Platinum Rule simply stated is; Do onto others as they would have you do onto them. In other words, treat other people the way they want and need to be treated. And that is the way that you can develop rapport with people quicker, deeper and longer lasting.*

### Mick Moore – The Internet Entrepreneur ™

*The Law of Attraction simply states like attracts like. What you focus on the most, you will attract into your life. The problem is that too many people focus on what they don't want instead of what they do want. They spend their entire lives running away from the bad instead of running toward the good.*

*How many times have you caught yourself thinking, "Why do I always get stuck in the longest line in the grocery store?" Or, "This always happens to me." Or, "I knew that was too good to be true."*

*By doing this, you are programming yourself with negative information. If a situation seems to go against you tell yourself, "Hey, this is actually working in my favor. I may not know how or why but I know that it is working in my best interest." Say this to yourself as many times as you need to in order to get back on track.*

*You never know, that little extra wait at the supermarket may have just saved you from being involved in the automobile accident you just passed on your way home from the store.*

### Marie Diamond – Feng Shui Master

*As an old lawyer, I can tell you laws are principles that work for everyone and the Law of Attraction works perfectly each time you use it. Each time you apply it, you will actually be able to attract your dreams.*

*The vision you want to establish in your life is about connecting with the vibration of what you want to focus on. Don't just focus on what you want to accomplish; focus on the vibration, the energy that it is.*

*If you want success, connect with the vibration of what success is. If you want love, connect with the vibration of love, and experience that vibration in your body, in your spirit, in your mind and experience what it really does to you.*

*The moment that you experience and feel it, you will start radiating out and the universe will bring it in, very gently, at the right moment, the right place and with the right people.*

### Marc Accetta, CEO – Marc Accetta Seminars
*In America, our Constitution guarantees us life, liberty and the pursuit of happiness. And while that is good, obviously, I think the pursuit part is where a lot of people get messed up.*

*Pursuit of happiness means we are chasing things we want. When we feel good, is it that we are attracted to someone? Or, are we attracted to someone because they are chasing us around all day long? Hardly!*

*What you find out is when you are chasing something it goes further away from you. It is like swimming after a ball in a pool; it just keeps getting further and further away. We need to learn how to stop pursuing things and start attracting them.*

### Bob Proctor, Best Selling Author –
You Were Born Rich

*You know, we talked about our dream, we talked about desire, we talked about vision and we talked about right thinking. Now we are going to talk about the Law of Attraction.*

*You know, the Law of Attraction is a secondary law; a lot of people talk about it but a lot of people don't really understand it. It's a secondary law; you attract according to the vibration you are in. The Law of Vibration is the primary law, and you vibrate according to your thoughts.*

*You see, all the great leaders have agreed that we become what we think about. We truly do become what we think about. They have disagreed on virtually everything else, but on that one point they are completely, unanimously in agreement.*

*We become what we think about. That is why right thinking is so important. As we become emotionally involved with our thoughts, they control the vibration we are in.*

*You see, your body is a molecular structure. This body is a mass of energy in a very high rate of vibration. If you were to put your body in front of an infrared television camera in a completely dark room, you would see that you are nothing but a gleaming, radiating form. As you change your thoughts, the vibration you're in, changes.*

*Way back in the 30's, a man named Semyon Kirlian, perfected Kirlian photography. It enables you to actually photograph the energy leaving the body. As you change your thought in your consciousness, the vibration you are in, changes.*

*I want you to think for a second. What is coming into your life? Pay attention to the people that are coming into your life, the thoughts that are coming into your consciousness, the things that are happening to you. You are attracting everything. You attract by virtue of the vibration you are in.*

*Now think of this! When we are consciously aware of our vibration, we don't say we are consciously aware that we are in a positive or negative vibration.*

*We say, "I feel good." Or, "I feel bad." Feeling is conscious awareness of our vibration. So we want to get involved in right thoughts. Get emotionally involved; that will control the emotion you are in. That dictates what you attract. You attract like energy. The people you are attracting are like you, they think like you. The thoughts you're attracting are in harmony with you and if you don't like what is coming into your life, change your thinking. Get really involved emotionally with your dream and when you do that just know that the whole universe operates in an orderly way.*

*Dr. Wernher von Braun, who is the father of the space program, said that "natural laws of this universe are so precise that we don't have any difficulty building space ships. We can send people to the moon and time the landing within a fraction of a second." He also said that these laws must have been set by someone. That is a subject for another time.*

*But understand this; you are in a high rate of vibration right now and, whether it is positive or negative, it will dictate what you will attract. Think about what you want to attract and begin to get into that vibration. The Law of Attraction is very important. It is everything.*

# Chapter 6

## Associations

As the company president watched his young student absorbing all this information, he noticed that Alonzo was not taking notes. He said in a stern voice, "Alonzo, you are not even taking notes."

This forceful statement jolted Alonzo from his thoughts and he replied, "I never liked taking notes in school; it seemed like a lot of work."

Disturbed by this reply, the mentor exclaims, "Alonzo, taking notes is very important. Taking notes is the first step to becoming an effective leader. Now listen; nobody wants to follow a leader who doesn't know where he is going.

"Leadership is nothing more than developing those associations around you; the people that you surround yourself with. Those people become your mentors, your teachers, your friends, and your clients.

If you don't get anything else I tell you in this entire conversation tonight, remember this; who you listen to will determine what you get, what you have and where you are going, and that is the truth.

"Look at the people around you and ask yourself, "Is this the team that will lead me to my dream?" If the answer is no, you need a new team."

## Master Mentors on Associations

### Mick Moore – The Internet Entrepreneur™
*The people you are associating with are either building you up or they're tearing you down. There are some people who are so supportive they leave you feeling like you can do just about anything. Then there are others who are so consumed by their own self doubt that, over time, they start to rub off on you and you will become discouraged.*

*My wife and I changed the group of friends we were associating with and almost immediately we started attracting a new group of friends with the same positive outlook in life we had. We were amazed at the increase; not only in the positive results in our lives, but our bank account reflected a major increase, as well.*

*Now, I am not suggesting you dump all your friends, just surround yourself with the ones who truly support your dreams and aspirations.*

### DC Cordova – Money & You ®
*Mentors will teach you principles, tools, and give you information from all their learning experiences and the mistakes they have made; learn from them!*

*Then, surround yourself with people who ask more of you than you ask of yourself. They not only support you, they also give you feedback. People are either supporting you in reaching your goal or holding your back from your magnificent destiny.*

*La hente te estan apoyando realizar, tu mentos o alejando tus metos de tu destino magnifico.*

### Dr. Peter J. Pizor – Author

*Ideas live within us and they only take shape and form when we speak them out loud. But the sound only has meaning when it is heard by someone. So there is a sequence for your words to have the power of convincing someone else; that someone else has to be there. Even more importantly, that someone has to be someone who can make a difference.*

*When you have an idea and you want to make a difference, think about it and put it into the most powerful words possible. Then share it with someone else. For that idea to really have an effect, to really change the planet, the people you share it with have got to be powerful in doing something.*

*Surround yourself with powerful people. The only difference between you today and you in five years will be the quality of your ideas, the power of the words you use to express them and the quality of the people that you are associated with.*

*From idea to word to association; together we can change this planet.*

**Marcia Wieder, Founder – DreamUniversity.com**
*The number one way to experience greater ease and short cuts to getting what you want is to share your dream with other people. Can you share your dreams with clarity so that people can get it? Express your dreams with passion so that people want to help you, and then, very clearly, make specific requests that make it easy for people to say yes.*

*Associate with great people who can help you get what you want and, most importantly, invite and inspire other people to join you. The way to do that is to make specific requests and make it easy for them to say yes. If they say no, ask them why. People often say no when we are asking for too much or they are not clear on what it is that you are asking for.*

**Lisha & Kari Schneider – Network Specialists**
**Kari** – *If anyone tells you they succeeded by themselves, they are probably not being completely honest. Even if you are super smart and work extremely hard, it is not enough, in today's world, to be successful. You need to build powerful partnerships, and powerful relationships .*

**Lisha** – *To succeed in life it is not just what you know, it's who you know supported by what you know; it's who you surround yourself with in your circle of influence. When the universe brings to you what you want and what you desire, it is usually through other people. You are as successful as the people you surround yourself with, who you associate with...*

### Kari & Lisha
*Who you associate with and keep as friends really makes a difference.*

### Dave Ulloa – Business Entrepreneur
*There is an old saying that goes, if you lie down with dogs you will wake up with fleas. But the opposite is also true, if you fly with eagles you will soar to levels you only dreamed about.*

*For example, if you were to take the five people you spend the most time with and average out their income, your income will be exactly the same, give or take about 5%. That also works for your health, relationships and level of success. The moral of the story is, carefully choose who you associate with because that could literally make a difference whether or not you succeed in your life and your level of fulfillment.*

**Dr. Tony Alessandra, Author** – The Platinum Rule
*One of my mentors, Charlie 'Tremendous' Jones, is
fond of saying the person you are today, verses the
person you will be five years from now, is a result of
the books that you read and the people you associate
with.*

*So, I propose you associate with people who really
want to see you succeed, that you are in the middle of
things, that you have mentors and role models above
you and you have people, mentees or protégés below
you who see you as their mentor and role model; not
people who are winners or losers. Associate with
winners and keep in touch with them, share ideas
with them.*

**Lisa Mason DiSalvo – Motivational Speaker**
*One of the most important things that you can do for
yourself in achieving success in your life is to have
great associations.*

*Did you ever notice you can hang out with certain
people and when you walk away you just feel great and
you want to conquer everything there is to conquer
in life and you feel good? These are the people that
make you feel like you can look at a mountain and
you can climb that mountain; you can get to the top
of that mountain. Not only have you achieved that
goal but you are looking around at a whole world of*

*more goals that you want to go after. Those are the people you want to hang around with.*

*So, when someone new comes into your life just think, is this that person that can take me to the top of that mountain? Those are the people to keep in your life!*

### Bob Proctor, Best Selling Author –
You Were Born Rich
*I want to ask you a question! If you had children, would you want them to grow up to be like the people you associate with? A lot of people will say no! But if you have children that is probably what is going to happen. You see, the people you associate with have a lot to do with who you are.*

*You know Karl Menninger from the Menninger Foundation down in Topeka once said, "Environment is more important then heredity." And he is right! The people we associate with have a greater bearing on where we are going in our life than what is built into our genes at birth.*

*Charlie 'Tremendous' Jones is a wonderful human being. He stated that we are nothing but the books that we read and the people we associate with.*

*I have a friend, Jane, that runs a large seminar company on the west coast, and she says she doesn't want to associate with anyone that doesn't think she is special. When she said that, I thought, "Wow!" But then I thought about it. I thought, "She is right! Why would I want to associate with anybody who doesn't think I'm special?" You see, if they don't think you are special then they don't think that they are special. They are probably involved in the wrong ideas, the wrong thoughts and you are picking up their energy when you are around them.*

*Now I am very selective about the people I spend a lot of time with. I want to spend time with people who are right thinkers, who are dreamers. They are into big ideas, they want to make something enormous happen in their life. By mixing with them I am picking up their thoughts.*

*Pay attention to the people you are associated with, think about them and think about the people you would like to associate with, and then become friends with them.*

*There is no trick to building friends. Be friendly, that's how you do it. The people you associate with are very important to you.*

The Power of Mentorship - The Movie

# Chapter 7

## Action

For the first time in his life, Alonzo realized that he really can become one of the successful. This knowledge gives him the courage to look at his mentor and ask, "Mr. Boyer, do you think you could help me get started with the things you just taught me? I really want to make a change in my life!"

Realizing that Alonzo is just getting the tip of the iceberg of knowledge, Mr. Boyer tells him, "Alonzo, you can know all the success principles in the world; you could read every book on success but if you never take any action on your dreams, nothing will ever happen. You see, action is what produces results. If you show me your results I can tell you what your actions have been."

## Master Mentors on Action

### Dr. Letitia Wright – Wright Place TV Show Host
*Even if you are not sure what to do, you need to take one step. Just start your actions, start putting things in motion. You will find out pretty soon whether or not it is the right thing to do. But you have to start by taking at least one step.*

### Yvette Ulloa – Business Entrepreneur
*To bring our dreams to life, we have to take action. John Assaraf, one of my mentors, once told me that if it was just about knowledge and information every librarian in the world would be a millionaire.*

*It is the application of information that creates true results. The action steps that we take to reach our goals don't have to be quantum leaps. We are conditioned to want instant results and we are disappointed if that doesn't happen. It is those simple action steps, simple actions of discipline, that compound over time to create massive success.*

*Think right now what it is that you want to achieve. What is an action step that you can take this very minute to get closer to achieving the outcome? Then, take that first step and take action now!*

### Mick Moore – The Internet Entrepreneur ™
*Taking action simply means being 100% committed to your goal and spending an amount of time each day working on that goal. You must expect positive results in order to achieve positive results. Winners expect to win and losers expect to lose.*

*Vincent Lombardi, one of the greatest football coaches of all time said, "We never lose but sometime the clock just runs out on us."*

*If you can believe it you can achieve it. Taking action starts by living that dream every single day.*

### DC Cordova – Money & You ®
*To have the life and business you want you must have a clear plan of action, then take action on that plan. Everyday, do at least five things from your plan toward your goals. You will find that it is those little steps that will bring big results into your life.*

*Vas aver que los pasos pequeños te van a traier grandes resultados en tu vida.*

### Melinda Boyer, CEO – Real Life Teaching Inc.
*Taking action in everything you do will result in getting everything you want in your life. Start taking the steps to take the action and you will have the result that you are looking for.*

### Robin Jay – *Motivational Speaker*
*Ask yourself where you want to be five years from now because it is what you do today that will make that difference.*

*Fear has a tendency to keep people where they are and there is really nothing to be afraid of. Ask yourself what is the worst case scenario? The odds are the worst scenario is that the worst case scenario will never come to pass.*

*Resolve to remove any road blocks that are in the way of you and your dream, and remember to do what you love. That way, you will love what you are doing everyday.*

### Stephen DiSalvio – *Motivational Speaker*
*Several years ago, one of my mentors introduced me to a line from a poem. The line is, to fill the unforgiving minute with 60 seconds of long distance running. The unforgiving minute is that period of time you let slip away without working toward your goals.*

*I had the opportunity to meet a gentleman several years ago; a good athlete. Everyday he is in the gym, he is working out, and I asked him—his name is Earl—"Earl, do you ever feel like not going to the gym?*

*"Do you ever feel like not working out?"*

*His answer was, "Of course!"*

*"Well then, what do you do?"*

*He said, "I simply put my shoes on. Putting my shoes on sparks me and gets me up and moving."*

*So the next time that you are unfocused, or the next time you are working on your dream and you really don't feel like doing what needs to be done or you don't think you can, just put your shoes on; take that action, and you will achieve your goal.*

**Dr. Tony Alessandra, Author** – The Platinum Rule
*I am a big advocate of that old Nike quote, "just do it."*

*Perfectionism paralyzes—paralyses by analysis— and it is especially true when you have a big task. You put it off, you procrastinate. Turn great big tasks into small tasks and just do it. My mother was fond of saying to me, "Don't go the extra mile, go the extra inch." It is a lot easier.*

**Bob Proctor, Best Selling Author –**
You Were Born Rich
*You know, I have been in the business I am in now and teaching these ideas for 39 years. I have traveled all over the world—our company operates all over the*

*world—we literally train people to teach these ideas in our company. I have seen a lot of people study this information. They have great libraries of CD's, and books, and hang out with people that love discussing this but they don't do anything; nothing is happening in their life. They honestly think that if they just talk about it long enough, it is going to happen.*

*Well, they are wrong! Talking about it doesn't make it happen.*

*I love the saying that the Quakers have, they say, "Pray and move your feet." You have got to get up and get out there and make it happen. If you stop and think about the people that are really the producers in this life and watch them, their days are busy. They have a long list of goal achieving activities and they get out and make them happen. They don't wonder what they are going to do when they get up in the morning; that was decided before they went to bed.*

*I am not saying they don't go to the cleaners or maybe drop into the bank or pick up bread on the way home from work, and I am not say they don't go out to the theater or associate with people; they do those things. But they have a list of activities everyday that are goal achieving activities and they have those all decided before they go to bed at night.*

84

*I want to make certain that you really understand this; you have to know what you are going to do tomorrow before you go to bed tonight. Get your mind to work achieving goal activities.*

*You see, some people accomplish more in a week then other people do in a year. Some people accomplish more in a month then some people accomplish in a life time. I do more in a month now than I did the first 26 years of my life! Why? I do it because I am following the process that you are learning. It is very important that you are active. Get into action!*

The Power of Mentorship - The Movie

# Chapter 8

## Believe

"Okay, I have shared seven things with you for your pathway to success," the company president tells Alonzo while looking him straight in the eye.

Then he says, "There is one more thing that you need; one last principle. It is, you have to believe. When nobody else believes in you, when no one else is going to believe in your dream, you have to believe in your dream.

"You have to have faith; and faith, Alonzo, is nothing more than your ability to peer into the invisible so that you can grasp on to that which is incredible, so that you can go out and do what all the masses say is impossible. Now, that is what faith is."

## Master Mentors on Believe

### Dr Letitia Wright – Wright Place TV Show Host
*You have to be the keeper of the flame. You can't hire anyone to do that and you can't delegate that job. It is about absolute faith. You have to believe more than anyone else.*

### Yvette Ulloa – Business Entrepreneur
*Once upon a time, there was a young girl who didn't believe in herself. She wanted more out of life but didn't quite believe she could have it or that she deserved it. Then came a mentor that told her anything was possible and believed in her more than she believed in herself. It was at that point that a seed of belief was planted which sprouted into a beautiful blossom of faith and love.*

*Thanks to that angel who believed in me, my life has been blessed with great success and abundance. And so, how do we create that belief in ourselves? By focusing on your faith and the endless realm of possibilities.*

*One of my mentors taught me that if we do what we fear the most, then the death of fear is certain. It is then that we can start walking the journey of true abundance and fulfillment.*

### Melinda Boyer, CEO – Real Life Teaching, Inc

*With faith, you can do the impossible. If you believe in your dream, then it can lead you from a prison into a palace. It did it for a young man named Joseph, in the bible. If you believe in your dream, then no one can steal it from you.*

### Stephen DiSalvio – Motivational Speaker

*You have got to have a belief. You have to believe in yourself and that belief has to be strong. It needs to be powerful.*

*When you have a strong positive belief, that energy goes out into the universe and, like always, the universe response with abundance. So, if your belief is positive, good, negative, or bad, what ever it is, you are going to get the same response, no matter what.*

*A French General once said, "There is not a weapon on earth more powerful then the human soul on fire." Catch fire! Get out there and positively believe and the universe will be your ally.*

### Marie Diamond – Feng Shui Master

*Belief is made up of two words: BE – LIFE! It is about being in the life you really wish for from the moment you start your day till the moment you go to sleep and even beyond that; into your dreams. Everything you do; your actions, your thoughts, your feelings, your spiritual experiences—everyday—it comes from the belief that you want to accomplish something.*

*It is very important that you act on it, you live it, in everything you do! Your thoughts, your feelings, your actions, your spiritual experiences; it has to be from that belief in yourself and knowing whatever people say about you or about what you want to accomplish, is their ideas. It is their belief systems.*

*You just have to focus on yourself and say this is what I believe, this is what I want to bring forward. You believe it for yourself and from then on you will experience that.*

*The world will start acknowledging and accepting your beliefs the more you believe in yourself. I can tell you the world will one day accept what you believe in. So, I tell you, live it! Believe It!*

### Marc Accetta, CEO – Marc Accetta Seminars
*In the Bible, it says if we have faith but as the size of a mustard seed, we can move a mountain. While it is understandable, I think a lot of people actually get that confused.*

*You see, our brains can only entertain one thought at a time. So, if we are thinking but a mustard seed of faith; it is all faith. However, if we have a mustard seed of doubt it is all doubt. So when life really starts coming to you, your goals will start being achieved very, very rapidly. That is when you get the concept.*

*When my life took off and things started working for me in every way possible, it is because I adopted one core system and that was, in order for me to go to where I wanted to get to, I had to have 100% total absence of doubt.*

### Machen MacDonald – Achievement Expert
*You have got to believe. To me, believing is having a high level of confidence knowing that you are going to achieve your vision. No matter what shows up, you may need to believe otherwise. We all need to have a level of belief.*

*What I like to do is play on the word confidence; break it up and spell it  CON FA DUNCE: CON means with, F, A is Frequent Affirmation —throughout your day affirm what you want and actually feel it!—it is when you are feeling as if you have already achieved it. DUNCE—spells dunce, and that means just be smart enough to be dumb enough to not worry about knowing it all before you get started; just go out there and do it.*

91

*Now, if you look at any success, there is way too much that just showed up. It was not planned or calculated; it just showed up when it needed to and you have to have faith in that and trust that. So if you have faith and know that it can happen, you will get what you want.*

*You know, unhappy, sick, broke people are under the illusion that they have to achieve something before they can feel happy or successful.*

*Well, happy, healthy, wealthy people just happily achieve and there is a world of difference. The choice you have to make is which world you want to live in.*

### Vic Johnson, Founder – AsAManThinketh.net
*In 1996, my family and I were evicted from our home. A year later, we lost the last automobile we had and in 1997, I earned so little money that I qualified at the Federal poverty level.*

*I realized I had to change something in my life. I scraped together as much money as possible during that time, and I made it to a seminar in Jacksonville, Florida. That evening, I heard from the stage, 13 magic words that changed my life:*

*The size of your success is determined*
*by the size of your belief.*
*The size of your success is determined*
*by the size of your belief.*

*Those words rocked my life, because I knew instantly that was the solution I was looking for. I knew instantly that was the piece of the puzzle that I was looking for in order to put my puzzle together.*

*I began an earnest, diligent effort to change my belief and magical things started to happen. Over the next 90 days, I began to energize people and opportunities came into my life that hadn't been there before.*

*Within six months, I won an international sales contest and within a year I was making a six-figure income; several years later, a seven- figure income.*

*The power of belief is incredible. You cannot experience anything in life that you don't first believe. You can't experience something you don't believe. You will never be rich if you believe yourself poor, no matter how much money you have. You will never be poor if you believe yourself rich, no matter how little money you have. It is all in the power of belief.*

## *Bob Proctor, Best Selling Author –*
You Were Born Rich

*You know, way back in 1900, William James, a great Harvard physiologist said, "Believe and your beliefs will create the fact."*

*If you look in the Bible, in the Koran, the Torah, any good book, every one of them will tell you, you've got to believe!*

*How do we develop beliefs? Well, the truth is most people don't. Most people inherit their beliefs. That is why they don't do much more than their parents, grandparents, and their great grandparents and you see a long string of people that all do the same thing.*

*I was doing that until I was 26. Then I picked up a book by Napoleon Hill and I read, "There is a difference between wishing for a thing and being ready to receive it." He said, "No one is ready to receive a thing until they can believe they can acquire it."*

*The state of mind must be belief and not your hope and wish. An open mind is essential to belief, a closed mind will not inspire faith, courage or belief. And he said, "Remember, it takes no more effort to demand abundance and prosperity in your life than it does to accept misery and poverty."*

*So, you see, the key factor here is BELIEVE! If you don't believe, then you are not ready. I also found, from another mentor of mine who said, "Our belief system is based upon our evaluation of something and frequently, if we re-evaluate a situation, it will change."*

*My income went from $4,000 a year to $175,000 a year and then it went over a million. I have earned millions of dollars. What happened? I hadn't gone to college, and I only had two months of high school, I had no business experience, if fact, I had a bad work record. But as I got into these books and the CD's and as I started to pay attention to my mentors and my coaches, what I really did was start to evaluate who I really was.*

*I got to the point that I was extremely fascinated with who I was. If you just study your body it will blow you away! Did you know that your mind is an electronic switching station? It is all just a vibration you are in that controls what you attract.*

*Did you know that the blood goes through 100 miles of passageway in your body every 33 seconds? It carries all the food in and all the garbage out, just like that, in one sweeping change. This is all happening and we are probably not even paying attention to it. How does that happen?*

*It happens because there is something phenomenal about you and about me and as we start to study it, do you know what happens? Our beliefs about what we are capable of doing changes. My belief about who I was and what I was capable of doing changed.*

*You see, I thought I was my name, but I am not really Bob Proctor. That is my name—that is not me. This is my body. You have never heard anyone phone in and say, body not coming in today, it is sick.*

*You know, there is something phenomenal about you; you are God's highest form of creation. And, as you study, you are going to start to believe new things about yourself. As you believe, it will be done. You see, your beliefs are very important. Remember what Hill said, "An open mindset is essential to beliefs." You have got to be prepared to throw away some of your most cherished beliefs when you learn something new about yourself.*

*Remember where I started; very few people develop beliefs; most inherit them. You have got to have real strong reasons for all of your beliefs and as you start to think you will start to see a lot of your old beliefs fall away. And you are going to believe in you. There is something phenomenal about you—and about me. Let's make sure we show that in our actions and the results that we are getting in our lives.*

96

# Chapter 9

## Mentorship

Alonzo finds he has such a strong feeling of excitement that he wants to rush out and put everything he has just leaned into action. Once again, he poses the question to his mentor. "Mr. Boyer, do you think you could help me get started with everything you just taught me? I really want to make a change in my life."

The mentor, now fighting hard to hold back his tears, looks away for a second and says, "You know, Alonzo, you are a sharp young man. I really think you have a lot of potential and you have a great future ahead of you. I do want to help you. I am going to give you this book and I want you to read it. Then I want you to come to my office once a week and we are going to go over these eight steps. Can you do that, can you commit to that?"

With his heart pounding, Alonzo says, "Most definitely! Thank you so much, Mr. Boyer." He stands up to leave the office.

## 3 Years Later

Looking out the window on the 34$^{th}$ floor of his office, we find a well dressed young man sitting behind his executive desk. He is being interviewed by *Business Now* magazine. The reporter asks the young man, "Well, Alonzo, are there any final comments you would like to make?"

Alonzo sits back and with a big smile says, "From janitor to business entrepreneur; I did it, so can you... Now, go find yourself a mentor!"

Turning off his desk light, ready to go home from a long day at the office, Alonzo finds the office janitor coming in to empty his trash. As Alonzo gets up to leave, the janitor looks at him and says..."**Can I ask you a question?**"

## *Bob Proctor Summary*

*You are at the end of a series of phenomenal information. You have watched and listened to some of the greatest teachings in the world. If you were to hire these people, it would probably cost you millions of dollars to sit here with them and listen to all this incredible information.*

*Let me summarize for you; you can take all this information, you can gather it in your consciousness, you could write an exam on it and pass the exam and change nothing. Why do you think there are so many brilliant people wandering the streets who are broke? Think of the people that are leaving school with phenomenal degrees and they never make anything happen.*

*You and I have been programmed. We are programmed genetically and then we are programmed environmentally. As infants, our subconscious mind is wide open and whatever is going on around us goes right into our subconscious mind. As these ideas go into our subconscious, over and over and over, through repetition they start to become fixed in our subconscious.*

*Let me explain a fixed idea; it is known as a habit. A habit is an idea that you act on without giving it a conscious thought. When you got up this morning, you just got dressed. You did not think of getting dressed, you might have thought about what you were going to put on but, whether you are going to wear clothes or not, never entered your mind—it is a habit.*

*When you sit down to eat you don't think about how you are going to get that food in your mouth, you automatically do it. You weren't born with this information. It is programmed into your mind; it is part of your conditioning.*

*Well, you and I have been conditioned. There are a multitude of habits in our subconscious mind. When you pull all the habits together, it is called a paradigm. A paradigm is a multitude of ideas in your subconscious mind and if that paradigm doesn't change, nothing is your life will change.*

**God Bless you!**
**This is Bob Proctor**
**Thank you**

# Bonus Chapters

## Dr. John Demartini - Best Selling Author

We are here to desire and grow in all areas of our lives: spiritually, mentally, vocationally, financially, with our families, socially and physically. We are here to expand all of these areas. Nobody gets up in the morning and wants to shrink. We all want to expand; it's natural.

The key, though, is to set our desires and our objectives according to our highest values. Every individual has a set of values. There are high values: discipline, responsibility, focus, inspiration and dedication and lower values; procrastination, frustration, hesitation, inertia. There is order in higher values and disorder in the lower.

When we respond to our higher values we become inspired but if we give in to the lower values then we require outside motivation. Make sure that you are setting goals and pursuing dreams that follow your desires and that they are truly the ones that are most congruent to what is most meaningful and purposeful for you. Be sure these goals are the ones you truly want. If you do this, then no one will ever have to get you up in the morning. You will love what you do and do what you love.

When I was 17 years old, I was in the Sunset Recreation Hall on the north shore of Oahu. I was a long-haired hippy surfer guy. I had the opportunity to meet Paul Bragg, who became a mentor of mine. He lectured for 45 minutes and after he finished, after an absolutely inspiring lecture, he gave us an opportunity to scan our lives and think about what we wanted to dedicate our lives to.

He said, "Whatever you set our mind to tonight, that would become your destiny." Ever since that night and that vision, I have been focused on what I am doing today. Now, almost 35 years have gone by and I love what I do. I do what I love.

There is no doubt that when you capture an inspiring vision, one to which you want to dedicate your life, your life unfolds opportunities and literally synchronizes and attracts into your life, people, places, things, ideas, and events that will help that vision become a reality. I can't tell you how inspiring it is to actually be blessed with that experience.

# Bonus Chapter - Dr. John Demartini

Ever since that time when I was 17, I have wanted to share this with other people and help other people get their vision. I assure you, if you go inside with a state of gratitude, close your eyes and ask your inner self to guide that vision and unfold it, an amazing vision will be revealed. You have that power inside you; to go out and do something extraordinary that can take you on a journey for 35 years.

Follow the vision of your heart that inspires you; that will transform the world and you deserve this because that is what you are designed to do; to do something creative and something magnificent and something inspiring for planet earth. There is no reason for playing small. Follow a great vision and you will have a great life.

The Power of Mentorship - The Movie

## Gerry Robert
### Best Selling Author, *Millionaire Mindset*

Have you ever asked yourself, what if you could have the income of your dreams? What if you could have the house of your dreams, the relationships? Someone told me that. A mentor told me that; that I could have in a month what I used to earn in a year.

You see, there is nothing wrong with winning. There is nothing wrong with wanting to go to the top. Decide that is what you are going to go after; fuel your dreams, fuel your desires by getting a mentor and doing exactly what he or she says.

In fact, those people who win the most in life are people that keep dreaming; keep their eyes on something irrespective of their life and the challenges, irrespective of what has happened in the past. Just to dream and keep dreaming and keep your eyes on what it is that you want even if you don't know how to get there. The real winners are dreamers.

The Power of Mentorship - The Movie

## Paul Martinelli
### President – Life Success Consultants

Right thinking requires that we have a shift in awareness; a shift in our perception. It requires that when we begin to look at certain conditions and circumstances in our life we have to begin to choose a different thought; a better thought. A mentor looks at your potential and guides you through that process.

The biggest gap in our lives is the gap between that which we know and that which we do. You can ask somebody who wants to improve their results to write down a list of three things that they know they can do, know they should do and know that if they would do it, it would improve their results. Most people have no problem writing down those three things.

If you asked them, "Why aren't you doing them?" they say, "I don't know!"

It requires action if we are going to change our results. Ultimately, you have to do the action necessary to change and improve.

The mentors in my life had the ability to look at the potential inside me that I was completely unaware of. I had always been conditioned or programmed to believe that the results in my life were a reflection of my potential and they really weren't.

The results that you and I get in our lives are a reflection of our awareness of our potential. What a mentor does is to identify that potential and draw it out of us.

You see, I think potential is something that we have all been conditioned or programmed to see; something *outside* of us. We think if we get a good education, that education has potential. If we get a good job, maybe the company has good potential, or maybe a certain person has potential. The truth is, all of those things provide opportunity.

All the potential there ever was or ever will be, you have. You have infinite potential and what a good mentor does is to identify that potential and draw it out of you.

# Bonus Chapter

## The Next Step
By Don Boyer

If you asked the average person what is the secret to getting rich, many would say, "You must go in early and stay late so that someday you can go in late and leave early."

In other words; Hard Work.

Unfortunately, that is a demented plan that rarely works. Some of the hardest working people I know struggle from pay check to pay check, and some of the richest people I know are always on an exotic vacation!

Right now, millions of people are living in their dream home, driving their dream car, married to their ideal mate and living the life of their dreams. Isn't it your turn to start living your dreams?

When my mentor posed that question to me many years ago, I thought in my mind, "Hell, yes, it's time!" But there was just one problem; I did not know what my next step was to get there. I did not know how to do it.

In those days my life was completely upside down. I was financially broke—ok, financially challenged—driving a broken down old car with nothing to show in the way of material success. I stayed in that condition until I learned the Secret; the secret of the Science of Getting Rich.

You see, there is a hard way and an easy way to life. The question is, "Which way will you choose?"

97% of people choose the hard way, not because they want to but because they are not aware of the easy way. My mentor, Bob Proctor, told me at breakfast one day, "People do not earn $100,000.00 a year because they want to, they earn $100,000.00 a year because they do not have the awareness to earn that much in a month."

**The Hard Way**
The hard way, which I used myself for many years, is to work hard, save every penny you can, fight your way to the top, sacrifice, and never give up.

Well, that is a fine plan to build an ulcer in your stomach, but not the plan to get rich. That is trying to create success from without. The secret to all success and all wealth is to learn to live your life from within, which is...

**The Easy Way**
Struggle, sacrifice and hard times are not necessary to become rich, but in fact, will cause riches to flee from you. The truth of the matter is, you can be, do and have anything you desire and have it all come to you without pain, struggle or distress.

I know this may sound crazy to you and be something you may have a hard time conceiving of, let alone believing. However, I assure you it is all true. The best news is, we can teach you how to do this.

Let me ask you a question; "Is the plan of hard work, sacrifice, scrimping and saving bringing you the riches and success you want? If the answer is no, then, my friend, you need a new plan.

Working hard on things that don't work, doesn't make them work!

If you want to change things around in every aspect of your life, if you truly want to become financially rich...the easy way, then you must learn The Science of Getting Rich. In order for you to learn this system it will require three things:

1. You must be willing to invest in yourself. If you do not invest in yourself you cannot possibly think that anyone else will invest in you.

2. Time: it will require you to take some time out of your busy day to invest in learning this easy to understand system.

3. You must take action. Stop making excuses for why you cannot take action and just do it.

If you are sick and tired of being sick and tired, of not reaching your dreams, and you want to really become financially Rich, than go to my personal website

www.ThePowerOfMentorship.TheSGRProgram.com

to see how you can now learn The Science of Getting Rich for yourself.

You are only a click away from learning the Secret to having all the money and freedom you could possibly desire.

Do you want to live the hard way and never get what you really desire?

Or the easy way and get everything you want?

The Choice is yours...choose well my friend!

www.ThePowerOfMentorship.TheSGRProgram.com

The Power of Mentorship - The Movie

# Master Mentor Biographies

## Don and Melinda Boyer

 Don Boyer is a national speaker, has authored three mega selling books, and is the creator of the best selling *The Power of Mentorship* book series. With power, passion, and purpose his mission is to share with people "Who they are, what they can become, what they can do, and what they can have." Having a proven track record in coaching, Don Boyer has helped a number of companies hit the million dollar a year mark. He has been paid up to $4000.00 per employee to help them reach their selling potential and goals.

Along with his published books, he also has a number of best selling teaching CD's in which he addresses the areas of success and personal development. One of his all time best sellers is his "Professor Series" DVD's. The Professor is a wacky, colorful character Don Boyer created and plays, teaching the science behind success.

Along with her husband, Melinda is an accomplished author and speaker, as well as co-founder and CFO of their company, Real Life Teaching. Don and Melinda are proud parents and grandparents of 9 children and 8 grandchildren.

Visit Don and Melinda Boyer online at www.DonBoyerAuthor.com

## Bob Proctor

For 40 years, Bob Proctor has focused his entire agenda around helping people create lush lives of prosperity, rewarding relationships and spiritual awareness.

Bob Proctor knows how to help you because he comes from a life of want and limitation himself. In 1960, he was a high-school dropout with a resume of dead-end jobs and a future clouded in debt. One book was placed in his hands – Napoleon Hill's *Think and Grow Rich* – which planted the seed of hope in Bob's mind. In just months, and with further support from the works of Earl Nightingale, Bob's life literally spun on a dime. In a year, he was making more than $100,000 and soon topped the $1 million mark.

It doesn't matter how you grew up, or what you've struggled with in life—your mind is unscathed by any circumstance you've struggled with in life—your mind is unscathed by any circumstance you've yet lived... and it's phenomenally powerful!

Let Bob Proctor's live seminars, best-selling books and recordings show you how to excavate the wonderful gem of your own mind.

Visit Bob Proctor online at
www.BobProctor.com

## Marie Diamond

 Marie Diamond is an internationally known Feng Shui Master and has been practicing for more than 20 years, refining the knowledge given to her at an early age.

Born in Belgium, she was trained as a lawyer and criminologist and worked for the Belgian and European governments and then as a project manager for a multinational publishing company. She has training and experience in all forms of management including Human Resources, Marketing, Safety, and Sales.

She is part of the Transformational Leadership Council created by Jack Canfield, which includes such respected members as Bill Harries, John Gray, John Assaraf, DC Cordova, Paul Scheele, and many others.

She has been featured in several TV and Film projects including *The Secret* (2006), *I Married A Princess* (2005), and *The Jerry Hall Heaven and Earth Show* (2005).

Visit Marie Diamond online at www.MarieDiamond.com

## Mick Moore, The Internet Entrepreneur™

 Mick Moore, "The Internet Entrepreneur™" is an award-winning web designer, author, highly acclaimed internet marketing consultant, and key-note speaker. Mr. Moore is the author of the *Home Business Success Kit*, the *Ultimate Internet Business Bible* and *The Internet Entrepreneur™*. He is CEO of KillerGraffix, a prominent design and marketing group, as well as CEO of Pacifica Marketing Group, Inc., both based in San Diego.

What makes Mick Moore an Online Business Expert?
- Award-winning Web Designer
- Leading Search Engine Optimizing Expert
- Degree in Graphic Design and Communication
- Makes his living entirely using the same techniques featured in his books/seminars
- Co-Director and featured in the smash-hit *The Power of Mentorship* movie
- Featured in *The Power of Mentorship* book series
- Featured in *Wake Up... Live the Life You Love* book series
- Featured instructor for The Learning Annex

Mick Moore dedicates his time to helping people and small business organizations understand how they can aggressively compete in today's high tech Internet market. His clients include major hotels and restaurants, government agencies, bio tech firms, lawyers and doctors. He has a proven track record delivering specialized marketing strategies for thousands of clients for over 10 years.

His Seminars and Boot Camps deliver incredible insider Tips & Tricks to creating a six-figure income online. His events are fun and exciting as he takes you step by step through the process of building your own successful internet empire and sharing the secret of *Turning Your PC Into a Paycheck.*

Visit Mick Moore online at
www.QuickStartExpert.com
www.TheInternetEntrepreneur.com

## Marc Accetta

 Marc serves as the President and CEO of Marc Accetta Seminars Inc., the Leading Edge Inc. and is the Founder of the Unstoppable Foundation. He is also the Director of Training for Liquidity International and WorldVentures Inc.

Marc graduated from Seton Hall University in 1982 and immediately began his career in sales. In his early years he was in the direct sales arena, regularly placing in his company's annual top 10 for personal sales. At 27 he decided to focus on developing sales teams as opposed to being a top salesperson himself. His entrepreneurial path ended up with him attending dozens of seminars on business and personal growth. That is where Marc's true passion came out. Marc's ability to build top producing sales teams is unquestioned. He has been at the top of his craft for 20 years, but his true excellence is in leading the types of seminars that he used to attend.

Marc's unique style is based on "Edutainment", which is the art of educating and entertaining his attendees at the same time. His signature seminar is called, A View From the Edge. In their latest project, Marc and his wife, Kelly, are bringing their dynamic training online.

Visti Marc Accetta online at
www.MarcAccetta.com.

## Dr. Tony Alessandra

 Dr. Tony Alessandra helps companies build customers, relationships, and the bottom-line. Companies learn how to achieve market dominance through specific strategies designed to outmarket, outsell, and outservice the competition.

Dr. Alessandra has a street-wise, college-smart perspective on business, having fought his way out of NYC to eventually realizing success as a graduate professor of marketing, entrepreneur, business author, and keynote speaker. He earned his MBA from the University of Connecticut – and his PhD in marketing from Georgia State University.

Dr. Alessandra is president of Online Assessments (www.OnlineAC.com), a company that offers online assessments and tests; co-founder of mentorU.com, an online e-learning company; and Chairman of the Board of BrainX, a company that offers online digital accelerated-learning programs.

Dr. Alessandra is a widely published author with 14 books translated into 17 foreign languages.

Visit Tony Alessandra online at www.alessandra.com

## Yasmine Bijan

 Yasmine is a Coach, Consultant, Speaker and Author. "Sculpt Your Business and Your Life Into a Masterpiece" is more than just a saying... it's her mantra. Yasmine understands that business and life are intertwined; you can't work on one without affecting the other. She is able to achieve greater results by targeting both areas for success. Her award-winning, unique approach to coaching is extremely effective and produces outstanding, spontaneous results.

Let Yasmine help you to "Sculpt Your Life" with her InPowerU Success Coaching program. You can contact her at 888-879-5338, or email her at yasmine@yasminebijan.com.

For more information, please visit www.yasminebijan.com.

The Power of Mentorship - The Movie

## DC Cordova

 DC is the CEO of the organization that has presented the world-famous Money & You® Program, the Excellerated Business Schools® for Entrepreneurs and other Excellerated programs since 1979. She continued with the work after the creators of the programs went on to develop other breakthrough technologies. She has had the honor of working and studying with some of the best business educators and entrepreneurs in the world, and has been involved in business and entrepreneurial education for nearly three decades. She is considered to be one of the pioneers of "New Education"—high-speed entrepreneurial business education.

She is considered a "Mentor of Nurturing" and works closely with top management teams and businesses to empower good relationships. She is an author of the comprehensive systems manual for entrepreneurs, *Money-Making Systems for People Who Work with People; The Power of Mentorship: The Millionaire Within* Book Series; and is currently writing *The Money & You® Book*. She has been a celebrity guest on several television shows and a guest speaker on many radio shows around the world.

She is an Ambassador of New Education and travels the world speaking with top business people, dignitaries, politicians, and persons of high influence. Her focus is promoting the transformation of educational systems so young people can then learn to handle money, business and life from an early age and ensure their success as adults.

Visit DC Cordova online at
www.exellerated.com

## Dr. John Demartini

 Dr. John Demartini is a world leading inspirational speaker and author at the forefront of the burgeoning personal and professional development industry. His scope of knowledge and experience is a culmination of 34 years of research and studies of more than 28,000 texts into over 200 different disciplines ranging from psychology, philosophy, metaphysics, theology, neurology and physiology.

Born in Houston, Texas, Dr. Demartini was one of two children. At the age of seven he was told he had a learning disability and would never read, write or communicate. At 14, he was a high school drop-out living on the streets and panhandling for food to survive. After a near death experience at 17, due to severe strychnine poisoning, Dr. Demartini made a decision that would change his life forever.

Dr. Demartini has captured the attention of celebrities, international sport personalities, noted politicians and UN representatives as the result of a self help methodology he developed and coined as 'The Demartini Method' ®. Derived from a study of Quantum Physics.

'The Demartini Method ®' is now being studied in a number of Universities and presented to psychologists, psychiatrists, social workers, health professionals and prison workers all over the world.

Visit Dr. Demartini online at www.DrDemartini.com

## Stephen and Lisa DiSalvio

 After spending several years in their respective careers as a speech-language pathologist and registered nurse, Lisa and Stephen became successful entrepreneurs with the launch of Cornerstone Real Estate Investors.

Their pursuit of real estate investing led them on a continuing journey of self-development and this journey inspired them to want to share their experiences and knowledge with others. To this end, they expanded their business ownership to include a second company, Firestarters, which strives to reach people through personal coaching and speaking events. As the French General in World War I, Ferdinand Foch, once stated, "There is no greater weapon on earth than the human soul of fire," and thus, the company name "Firestarters".

Lisa and Stephen have been mentored in Real Estate by Jon and Stephanie Iannotti, participating in their Financial Independence Network group and currently mentoring new real estate investors in the Iannotti's Real Estate Investors Teaching group. Lisa and Stephen are graduates of Greg Pinneo's Power Players program, The Bridge with Life Tigers, the Present with Purpose program with George Ramirez, and are also members of the Las Vegas Convention Speakers Bureau.

They are both co-authors in *The Power of Mentorship* book series including the recently published, *For the Woman Entrepreneur* and the upcoming edition, *For the Business Entrepreneur.*

Contact Lisa and Stephen at:
lisa.disalvio@yourfirestarters.com and
steve.disalvio@yourfirestarters.com

## Glenda Feilen

 Glenda Feilen, author, speaker, and recognized authority on the Law of Attraction, shares no-fail techniques to achieve prosperity and success in her book, *Are All Your Pieces In Place.*

For over 25 years her books, seminars, and workshops have taught thousands an empowering process to achieve wealth, happiness, and rewarding relationships based on the Law of Attraction.

Her mission is to show others how to employ simple, easy techniques to attract tremendous abundance and success in every aspect of their lives. She is a nutritional expert and has been a marketing director for over 25 years in an international nutritional based corporation.

Her 'Law of Attraction' workshops are life changing and fun, fun, fun!

Glenda's books include:
- *Life is a Puzzle! Are All Your Pieces in Place*
- *Three No-Fail Techniques*
- *Your Body Shape Shapes Your Personality*

- *10 Habits You Need to Succeed*
- *Law of Attraction 'Special Edition'*
- *For the Woman Entrepreneur*

Visit Glenda online at
www.AreAllYourPiecesInPlace.com

## Robin Jay

 Robin Jay worked as an Advertising Account manager more than 18 years. She experienced a 2000% increase in sales in her career, largely because of her ability to build strong, long-lasting relationships. During that time, Robin personally hosted more than 3,000 client lunches making her the undisputed 'Queen of the Business Lunch'!

Now, as a professional keynote speaker, award-winning author and corporate trainer, Robin is not just the 'Queen of the Business Lunch', but is a business relationship expert who shares the nuts-and-bolts of building profitable business relationships.

Jay's proven ability to communicate the laws of the universe in language that everyone can understand, to deliver messages that motivate and inspire her audiences in accordance with those laws, transforms her audiences through a journey of increased self-actualization and greater success, both personally and professionally.

Jay's books include: *The Art of the Business Lunch – Building Relationships Between 12 and 2* (Career Press, 2006). This award-winning book has been sold in ten languages worldwide, and is also available in Audio formats. *The POWER of Mentorship* series of books: *The Millionaire Within,For the Woman Entrepreneur,Chicken Soup for the Wine Lover's Soul.*

Visit Robin Jay online at
www.RobinJay.com

## Vic Johnson

Vic Johnson is a Ponte Vedra Beach, Florida-based Internet infopreneur, author, motivational speaker and founder of a host of personal development websites.

Formerly the founder of a corporate and political communications firm, he has provided strategic consulting and planning to Governors, Members of Congress, Fortune 500 companies and non-profit organizations. His non-traditional strategies have been highlighted by major news outlets like the *Miami Herald, Washington Post* and national trade publications.

Vic bought his first business at the age of 23 and several years later became one of the early pioneers of the 'quick-lube' business, building the first locations in Florida.

His latest ventures have been Internet-based where he has quickly demonstrated his entrepreneurial acumen. Talk show host Mike Litman called one of his sites, AsAManThinketh. net, "the hottest personal development site on the Internet today." Subscribers hail from more than 90 countries and have downloaded over 300,000 eBook copies of James Allen's classic. His other websites are found at MyDailyInsights. com, mp3Motivators.com, Goals-2-Go.com and VicJohnson.com.

Visit Vic Johnson online at
www.VicJohnson.com

## Machen MacDonald

 You are BRILLIANT! You just may not see it yet! However, I do. It's a matter of awareness.

As your coach, it's my job to see Your Brilliance and have you become aware of it for yourself. Once you do—then your potential is ignited! As this happens, you can then comfortably take the actions necessary to attract into your life all that you desire to experience.

As you gain clarity of what you really desire to have for yourself and stay focused, you become more attractive. Everything you could possibly want for yourself is already available to you. It's already out there! It then becomes about making yourself available to your goals, needs and desires.

As your coach, I can show you how simple it really is to become available and attractive to your most fantastic desires. Permit me, as your coach, to show you how.

Visit Machen MacDonald online at www.ProBrilliance.com

The Power of Mentorship - The Movie

## Paul Martinelli

 As Bob Proctor's teaching and business partner, Paul Martinelli shares the international stage and collaborates with Bob to teach people how to achieve their dreams. Paul is a dynamic entrepreneur and President of Life Success Consulting.

Before teaming up with Bob Proctor, Paul worked with Guardian Angels to bring safety and education to some of the most challenging neighborhoods in the United States.

Paul is a recipient of Northwood University's Entrepreneur of the Year award and has gained an international reputation as a public speaker and leader in the personal development industry.

Visit Paul Martinelli online at
www.LifeSuccessConsultants.com

The Power of Mentorship - The Movie

## Marvin Pantangco

 Marvin Pantangco DDS has spent his days Smiling his way to the top. Helping people smile by becoming a dentist, Dr. Marvin received his degree in Dental Surgery from Ohio State University and completed an additional year at the University of Texas Health Science Center – San Antonio. Then he opened his dream dental practice just outside San Antonio.

Dr. Marvin created one of the most high-tech dental practices in the country, blossoming into one of the nation's finest Cosmetic Dentists. He transformed teeth and gums into Hollywood Smiles—but he didn't stop there. Dr. Marvin soon realized that changing a person's smile also changed their life. When someone went through a smile makeover their self-image improved, they became more confident and their outlook on life became more positive and had more vigor.

Now, Dr. Marvin has taken his talents to California where his writings appears in books alongside the likes of Zig Ziglar, Jim Rohn, Brian

Tracy, and Charlie 'Tremendous' Jones.

Dr. Marvin now creates smiles with everyone he comes in contact with by guiding, advising, and empowering them to succeed. His current projects include producing his won Web Television Channel, creating the world's greatest Dental Information Website (www.SmileIQ. com), and developing products to benefit anyone who cares about their smile. (www.3minSmile. com).

Visit Dr. Marvin online at
www.DrMarvin.com.

## George Ramirez

 As a successful businessman, George has started 3 businesses, traveled to 35 U.S. states and 26 countries. As a recognized speaker, his ability to engage an audience and truly get the message across, is well known in the industry.

His affiliations and contributions include:
- Featured author in the entire *Power of Mentorship* book series
- Co-star in *The Power of Mentorship* movie
- Associate Producer and co-star in the movie *Pass It On*
- Member of the One Coach 'Business Mastery Group'
- Contributor to the 'Millionaire Mentor Team'

George focuses on training and coaching public speakers and presenters with his 'Present with Purpose' Boot Camps producing quality results for all attendees.

Visit George Ramirez online at
www.GeorgeRamirezAuthor.com

The Power of Mentorship - The Movie

## Gerry Robert

 Gerry Robert brought himself out of poverty to earning over $1 million in a single year. He's now a mentor to some of the highest income earners in numerous industries, speaking alongside Bob Proctor. He genuinely cares about people and is great at what he does. Gerry is the father of three boys and has been married for over 20 years to Anne, his teenage sweetheart. He is also a former minister.

He is a bestselling author, columnist, speaker and consultant operating throughout North America and Asia. Gerry has spoken to over one million people from around the world.

He has written several best selling books including *Conquering Life's Obstacles, The Magic of Real Estate* and *The Tale of Two Websites: A Conversation About Boosting Sales On The Internet, The Millionaire Mindset: How Ordinary People Can Create Extraordinary Income.*

Visit Gerry online at
www.GerryRobert.com

The Power of Mentorship - The Movie

## Lisha and Kari Schneider

 Lisha and Kari are so identical their own dad can't tell them apart. They've had fun doing the twin-switching thing. They've also enjoyed doubling their money and fun by working together.

The twins began in the entertainment field by being stunt and body doubles for Mary-Kate and Ashley Olsen. After several movies and television parts, they were introduced to the travel business, becoming top female income earners in less than a year!

Lisha and Kari have been featured in national magazines as highly successful entertainers and businesswomen entrepreneurs. They also are part of a successful Entertainment Distribution Company and authors of the book *Double Your Profits,* a step-by-step process on how to build a fast growing business in network marketing and become financially free.

Visit Lisha and Kari online at
www.TwinPower.biz

The Power of Mentorship - The Movie

## Dave and Yvette Ulloa

 Influential and nationally sought after speakers in success and personal growth, Dave and Yvette Ulloa have always excelled in an environment of challenge and transformation.

Yvette, along with her husband, Dave, have gone up the ranks to the top leadership of the fastest growing online travel company, World Ventures. Yvette and Dave were the recipients of the 2007 Business Mastery Award by John Assaraf, one of the featured teachers in the hit movie, *The Secret.*

Their empowering message about perseverance, determination, and the search for meaning in our lives has reached thousands of people around the world.

Contact Dave and Yvette at:
dave@vipdreamtrips.com and
yvette@vipdreamtrips.com

The Power of Mentorship - The Movie

## Marcia Wieder, CEO and Founder of Dream University®

 is leading a Dream Movement. With over twenty years coaching, training and speaking experience, her inspiring message, style and wit has touched audiences from 50 to 5000 at companies such as AT&T, The Gap and American Express.

Whether teaching at the Stanford Business School, speaking to executives in China, or addressing young women at Girl Scout Camp, her riveting style impacts audiences world wide. Marcia has appeared on *Oprah, The Today* show, in her own PBS-TV Special and has written several books and been translated into numerous languages. Her newest, *Dreams Are Whispers From The Soul*, was just released.

As past president of the National Association of Women Business Owners, she was often in the White House where she met former U.S. presidents, Ronald Reagan, Jimmy Carter and George Bush, Sr. And as a columnist for *Motto* magazine and *The San Francisco Chronicle,* she urged readers to take "The Great Dream Challenge."

Dream University® events include: the Dream Coach Certification program, the Inspiring Speaker Workshop, Create Your Future Now, Masters of Manifestation and the Visionary Leader Intensive. Her online global community, www.AmazingDreamers.com has thousands of members and networks dreamers world-wide.

Visit Marcia Weider online at
www.dreamuniversity.com

## Dr. Letitia Wright

 Dr. Letitia S. Wright, D.C. is the host of the Wright Place™ TV Show. The Show is now in it's 7th season with over 175 shows broadcast on television to over 3.8 million homes each week in Southern California.

The Wright Place™ TV Show is the fastest growing women's show about business on air today. Each episode features guests such as Mark Victor Hansen, Stedman Graham, Robert G. Allen, T. Harv Eker, Marie Diamond (*The Secret*), Rieva Lesonsky, John Assaraf (*The Secret*), D.C. Cordova, Teri Hatcher, Marla Gibbs, and Christina Ferrari, with discussions about strategies and new technology that women can use to grow their businesses.

Visit Dr. Letitia Wright, D.C. at
www.TheWrightPlaceTV.com

## Dr. Peter J. Pizor

 Dr. Peter J. Pizor helps his clients live extraordinary lives. While leading climbs in tough mountain terrain, he discovered the secret techniques that empower others to climb their own mountains and discover the success that awaits them at the summit. Peter served as chairman of a large non-profit with operations in 80 countries, a non-profit housing corporation and as a special consultant to Mary Holmes college in Mississippi. His dynamic communication skills have been recognized by two universities which named him Professor of the Year and by the National Speakers Association. He is president-elect of the Las Vegas Chapter, which named him "Member of the Year" for 2006.

To contact Peter, visit his website at www.pizor.com or telephone (702) 433-3989.